JARLSBERG DELIGHTS

Edited by
Ruth Marcussen Kielland
Norwegian Dairies Association

Photos:
Ragge Strand · Per Alfsen A/S
Food stylist: Ruth Marcussen Kielland
except
Norseland Food Inc.:
beer soup,
ham and onion pie,
The Jarlsberger,
quiche,
vegetable bisque,
stuffed fillets.

Jonas Friestad: Jarlsberg cheese making

Front and back paper photographs by
Husmo-Foto:
f) Lyngen, b) Geiranger

Second Printing

Printed by Aarhuus Stiftsbogtrykkerie, Århus 1986
ISBN 82-05-16906-3

JARLSBERG
CONTENTS

JARLSBERG CHEESE

A potted history

JARLSBERG cheese is exclusive to Norway. It was redeveloped in the early 1950's from an old formula used by Swiss cheesemakers who settled in Norway in the first half of the nineteenth century.

On the western shore of the Oslo fjord, leading to the capital of Norway, is an old estate with roots going back to the country's Viking era. Cheese was produced on this estate for many years before the Swiss moved in, and when the redeveloped cheese was to be named, it was natural that it should be given the name of the estate, JARLSBERG.

After the devastating years of World War II, when the milk supply in Norway was again adequate, Professor O. M. Ystgaard at the Agricultural University of Norway took an interest in widening the range of cheeses produced in the country. Using the formula mentioned above, he carried out numerous experiments and tests with the object of establishing the identity and characteristics of the cheese he thought the formula re-

presented. At the same time it was necessary to adapt production methods to modern dairy technology without losing the essential features of the cheese which make it so distinctive.

After five to six years of continuous research, studies and experimental production, the cheese was finally presented to the Norwegian public in the early 1960's.

Consumer acceptance was slow, but sure. This slow start made it possible for production to keep abreast of the demand, so that the Norwegian Dairies Association decided to introduce the cheese to export markets as well.

JARLSBERG cheese was first exported to Britain, the USA and Western Germany in 1963. Again, the markets developed slowly. Consumers in these countries were still conservative in their cheese-eating habits. Before the travel and tourist explosion, people stuck to their native foods. But in the early 1970's the demand suddenly soared, particularly in the USA. Since then about 12.000 tons of JARLSBERG cheese per annum have been exported to all corners of the world. In addition thousands of tons are sold on the domestic market.

Modern and efficient dairies have played a significant role in the success of JARLSBERG cheese on the world market, producing the all important uniform quality which has become the hallmark of the product and is a testimony to the skill and care of the cheesemakers.

Finally, and never to be forgotten, is the part played by the raw material, the milk. Norway is favoured with excellent grasslands where the cows thrive in sparsely populated areas and the rivers flow clear and clean from the mountain plateaux. Cool climate keeps the use of pesticides to an absolute minimum. Absence of serious animal diseases has enabled Norwegian dairy farmers to obtain premium prices, year after year, for the high quality milk they supply to the dairies.

Since its introduction on the world market during the 1960's and 1970's, the success of JARLSBERG cheese has encouraged the production of many imitations, some good, some bad. However, they all lack the attractive uniformity, the delectable nuances of flavour and aroma and the versatility in use of JARLSBERG cheese.

This book of recipes, with JARLSBERG cheese as a major ingredient, is designed to encourage the wider use of nourishing JARLSBERG cheese in the family diet.

We wish you "Bon appétit", good luck in experimenting with the recipes and enjoyment of the end results.

Yours sincerely,
NORWEGIAN DAIRIES ASSOCIATION

N B Kielland
Export director

JARLSBERG CHEESE

Around the clock around the world

- Breakfast in Stockholm
- Morning snack in Montreal
- Lunch in New York
- Afternoon tea in London
- Cocktail nibbles in San Francisco
- Dinner in Sydney
- Late night snack in Hamburg

Bon appétit
Guten Appetit
God appetitt

JARLSBERG THE TABLE CHEESE

The Jarlsberg is served.

Its appealing, big eyes are twinkling a little welcome to attack.

No food is more convenient. No cheese is more inviting. Put Jarlsberg on your table. Its distinctive nutlike flavour and soft texture will appeal to everyone.

Serve it simple, but elegantly. Give the cheese time to obtain the right temperature.

Use your favourite bread, biscuits, and a good knife …

Cut generous slices, and enjoy!

Jarlsberg Shrimp Salad

4-6 servings

2 cups Jarlsberg, cut in cubes – 200 g
1 cup cooked, peeled shrimps – 200 g
1 cup celery, diced – 2-3 dl
1/2 cup apples, diced – 1 1/2 dl
fresh lettuce
fresh dill

Dressing
1 cup light sour cream – 2 1/2 dl
2 tablespoons lemon juice
1 tablespoon ketchup
1 teaspoon sugar
1/4 teaspoon white pepper
2 tablespoons dill, chopped

Arrange all ingredients in one big bowl
or individual salad bowls. Mix dressing
ingredients and pour over. Garnish with
fresh dill and unpeeled shrimps. Serve
cold, with hot Jarlsberg bread.

Jarlsberg Crock

1 egg white, stiffly beaten
4 cups Jarlsberg, finely grated – 400 g
1 tablespoon oil
2 teaspoons Dijon mustard
¹/₂ teaspoon salt
2 cloves garlic, pressed
1 tablespoon Worcestershire sauce
1 cup dark beer – 2¹/₂ dl

To stiffly beaten egg white, add remaining ingredients except beer. Blend well. Add beer gradually while stirring until the mix has the consistency of a thick spread. Store in refrigerator in covered crock or other tightly covered container. If spread dehydrates, a little more beer may be added.

Serve as an hors d'oeuvre on small rye slices, thinly sliced baguettes, or use to stuff celery.
   Also makes a great sandwich spread and open-faced broiled sandwiches.

Jarlsberg Pumpernickel Surprise

Use a whole round pumpernickel bread. Slice off the top and save. Hollow out the inside saving it to cut cubes for dipping. Leave about ¹/₂ inch (1¹/₄ cm) shell and fill it with the Jarlsberg Crock mixture. Replace bread lid.

Wrap in aluminium foil and bake in a slow oven 250 °F. (120 °C) for 2 hours.

Unwrap, place on serving dish, surround with fresh vegetables, pumpernickel and white bread cubes. Provide fondue forks or long picks for dipping.

Jarlsberg Surprise Salad

6-8 servings

First layer:
2 cups salad greens, shredded – 5-6 dl
$^1/_2$ cup green onions, chopped – $1^1/_2$ dl
$^1/_2$ cup celery, sliced – $1^1/_2$ dl
$^1/_2$ cup red pepper, cut in strips –
    $1^1/_2$ dl

Second layer:
$1^1/_2$ cups green peas – $3^1/_2$ dl
$1^1/_2$ cups apples, cubed – $3^1/_2$ dl
$^1/_4$ cup lemon juice – over apples –
    $^1/_2$ dl

Third layer:
$1^1/_2$ cups sour cream – $3^1/_2$ dl
1 teaspoon Dijon mustard
1 teaspoon curry powder
1 tablespoon sugar

Fourth layer:
2-3 cups Jarlsberg, shredded – 200-300 g
1 cup crisp bacon, crumbled – 200 g

In large salad bowl arrange first and second layer. Mix ingredients for third layer and spread over salad to seal. Refrigerate overnight. Just before serving, sprinkle cheese and bacon on top.

Jarlsberg Melon Salad

4 servings

1 medium or 2 small honeydew
   or cantaloupe melons
2 cups Jarlsberg – 200 g
1 cup apples, cubed – $2^1/_2$ dl
1 cup celery, thinly sliced – $2^1/_2$ dl
$^1/_2$ cup red pepper, cut in strips –
   $1^1/_2$ dl
2 small sweet gherkins, diced
2 tablespoons lemon juice
crisp salad greens

Dressing:
$^1/_2$ cup sour cream – $1^1/_2$ dl
2 tablespoons lemon juice
$^1/_2$ cup blue cheese, crumbled – 50 g
1 tablespoon sugar

Cut melon in half. Remove seeds. Scoop
out and cube melon. Combine all ingredients including some salad greens.
Spoon salad into melons. Blend all ingredients for dressing. Serve over salad.

JARLSBERG THE SANDWICH CHEESE

Scandinavian SMØRBRØD are famous.

The word means buttered bread, and what really sets smørbrød apart is what goes on top of the bread.

PÅLEGG is a Scandinavian word, and pålegg means «something laid on».

Cheese plays an important role here – and cheese is used for millions of Scandinavian sandwiches every day. The Jarlsberg sandwich is a special one.

- open-faced with kiwi
- English sandwich with lettuce and ham
- baguette with mustard, lettuce and red pepper

Make the Jarlsberg sandwich your favourite.

Jarlsberg Pineapple Toast

Buttered bread, mustard, cooked ham, pineapple and Jarlsberg.

Put under the broiler or in hot oven 450 °F (225 °C) until cheese is golden.

Jarlsberg Bacon,
Apple Toast

In skillet cook bacon until crisp. In drippings cook apple segments until tender. Cover toast with a generous slice of Jarlsberg. Cook under the broiler until cheese melts.

Serve with bacon and apple.

Jarlsberg Mussel Toast

Buttered bread, pickled or cooked mussels, chopped onion, red pepper and parsley. Grated Jarlsberg on top.

Bake in hot oven 450 °F (225 °C) until bread is crisp and cheese is golden.

Jarlsberg Croque Monsieur

Cover one round of buttered bread with ham and cheese. Top with another round of bread. In skillet brown sandwich on both sides in butter.

Serve immediately.

Jarlsberg Club Sandwich

Crisp toast with layers of lettuce, tomatoes, gherkins, pepper, crisp bacon and Jarlsberg cheese.

The Jarlsberger

Whether you cook your hamburger medium or rare – top it with a large slice of Jarlsberg cheese. Give it another few seconds under the broiler, and you have a world favourite, the Jarlsberger.

JARLSBERG THE COOKING CHEESE

Cheese sauces, fondues, omelets, soufflés, soups – even scalloped potatoes will reach their utmost when made with Jarlsberg cheese.

It is important to cook the cheese rapidly and at medium temperatures. High temperature tends to make it stringy and rubbery.

The cheese is normally shredded, grated or diced to shorten the cooking time. Any left overs or dry cheese ends may easily be used in cooking. Remove the wax before shredding the cheese. Grated Jarlsberg may be frozen in small plastic bags, handy when a little grated cheese is needed instantly.

Cooking with Jarlsberg is fun – Good luck!

Jarlsberg Vegetable Bisque

6-8 servings

3 tablespoons butter
3 tablespoons flour
4 cups beef broth – 10 dl
1 cup broccoli, chopped – 2-3 dl
1 cup carrots, chopped – 2-3 dl
$^1/_2$ cup green onions, chopped – $1^1/_2$ dl
$^1/_2$ teaspoon thyme, crushed
$^1/_2$ teaspoon salt
$^1/_2$ teaspoon pepper
1 cup whole milk – $2^1/_2$ dl
2 cups Jarlsberg, shredded – 200 g

In saucepan, melt butter. Add flour. Gradually blend in broth. Bring to boil. Add vegetables, salt, pepper and milk. Cover, simmer for 8 minutes.

Blend in cheese. Serve immediately.

Jarlsberg Macaroni Bake

6 servings

1 pound ground beef – 500 g
2 tablespoons butter
1 cup mushrooms, sliced – 150 g
1 medium onion, chopped
$^1/_2$ cup red peppers, chopped – 2 dl
1 teaspoon salt
$^1/_2$ teaspoon pepper
3 tablespoons butter
3 tablespoons flour
$2^1/_2$ cups whole milk – 6-7 dl
2 cups Jarlsberg, shredded – 200 g
1 can tomatoes, chopped – 300 g
3 cups pasta, cooked – 300 g
1 can tomato sauce – 30 g

In skillet, brown beef in butter. Stir in next 5 ingredients. Cook until tender. Meanwhile melt butter, add flour, blend in milk. Cook, stirring until thickened and smooth. Stir in $1^1/_2$ cups cheese, tomatoes and pasta. Alternate layers of pasta and meat mixture in buttered dish. Top with tomato sauce.

Bake at 350 °F (170 °C) 30 minutes.
Top with remaining cheese.
Bake 5 minutes more.

Jarlsberg Beer Soup

6-8 servings

3 cups pale beer – 7$^1/_2$ dl
3 tablespoons chicken stock base
1 cup carrots, shredded – 2-3 dl
1 cup celery, thinly sliced – 2-3 dl
$^2/_3$ cup onions, thinly sliced and separated
   into rings – 2 dl
3 cups whole milk – 7$^1/_2$ dl
$^1/_3$ cup flour – 50 g
2 cups Jarlsberg, shredded – 200 g
salt and pepper

In large saucepan combine beer and chicken base. Heat until base is dissolved. Add vegetables and let simmer 10 minutes. Blend milk and flour. Blend into soup. Cook, stirring until thickened and smooth. Add cheese and let it melt in soup. Season with salt and pepper.

Jarlsberg Twist Bread

2 loaves

4 cups flour – 600 g
1 tablespoon sugar
1 teaspoon salt
1 package dry yeast
1 cup water – 2$^1/_2$ dl
$^1/_3$ cup milk – $^3/_4$ dl
$^1/_4$ cup butter, melted – 75 g
1 egg
$^1/_3$ cup parsley – chopped
3 cups Jarlsberg, shredded – 300 g

Mix dry ingredients. Heat water, milk and butter until lukewarm. Blend into dry ingredients. Add egg and 1 cup cheese. Knead dough until smooth. Cover and let rise until doubled.

Punch down and divide in half. Roll out two 12×15 inch (30×40 cm) rectangles. Sprinkle with parsley and remaining cheese. Roll up from short side. Cut in half lengthwise and twist together. Tuck ends under to seal. Cover and let rise to doubled.

Bake in preheated oven 400 °F (200 °C) for 20-25 minutes.

Jarlsberg Spice Sauce

4 servings

2 tablespoons butter
1 clove garlic, minced
1 teaspoon dill, chopped
  (¹/₄ teaspoon weed)
2 tablespoons flour
1 cup whole milk – 2¹/₂ dl
¹/₂ teaspoon salt
¹/₂ teaspoon Dijon mustard
dash of cayenne pepper
1¹/₂ cups Jarlsberg, shredded – 150 g

In saucepan melt butter. Add garlic and dill. Let simmer for 2-3 minutes. Add flour and gradually milk, stirring until thickened and smooth. Cook 3-5 minutes. Season with salt, mustard and cayenne. Finally add cheese, stirring until melted. Serve over fresh cooked vegetables.

Easy Cheese Sauce

4 servings

1 cup fine dry bread crumbs – 150 g
1¹/₂ cups whole milk – 3¹/₂ dl
1¹/₂ cups Jarlsberg, shredded – 150 g
¹/₂ teaspoon dry mustard
¹/₂ teaspoon salt
¹/₈ teaspoon pepper

In saucepan soak bread in milk for ¹/₂ hour. Combine with cheese and seasonings. Cook, stirring over low heat until cheese melts and sauce is smooth. Serve over fresh cooked vegetables.

Jarlsberg Salmon Sauce

In saucepan or oven cook your salmon steak in its own juice with just a little pinch of salt. In skillet sauté 2 tablespoons chopped onion (for 2 portions) in 1 tablespoon butter. Add 1 cup ($2^1/_2$ dl) cream, boil 10 minutes or until reduced to half amount. Add 1 cup shredded Jarlsberg, and let it melt in the cream sauce. Juice from the salmon steak may also be added.

Serve the salmon with asparagus, potatoes and the sauce.

Jarlsberg Green Beans

4-6 servings

2 tablespoons flour
2 tablespoons butter
1 cup sour cream – 2$^1/_2$ dl
1 teaspoon onion, grated
1 teaspoon salt
$^1/_4$ teaspoon sugar
2 pounds fresh green beans, cooked or
2 16 ounce cans green beans, drained –
   1000 g

2 cups Jarlsberg, grated – 200 g
$^1/_2$ cup almonds, slivered – 1$^1/_2$ dl

Melt butter, stir in flour and cook until bubbly. Stir in sour cream, onion, salt and sugar.

Place layers of green beans and cheese in greased casserole and pour sauce over. Top with almonds.

Bake at 350 °F (180 °C) for 20 minutes.

Jarlsberg Omelet

4-6 servings

$^1/_2$ cup mushrooms, sliced – $1^1/_2$ dl
$^1/_3$ cup green onions , sliced – 1 dl
3 tablespoons butter
6 eggs
6 tablespoons cold water
$^1/_2$ teaspoon salt
$2^1/_2$ cups Jarlsberg, shredded – 250 g
$^1/_2$ cup cooked ham, diced – 100 g
2 tablespoons parsley, chopped

In large skillet sauté mushrooms and onions in butter until onion is soft. In bowl beat together eggs, water and salt. Add to skillet. Add cheese evenly into omelet mixture. Sprinkle ham and parsley on top. Cook under cover without stirring 8-10 minutes over moderate heat. Lift to allow uncooked egg to run under. Cook until eggs are set and cheese is melted. Serve immediately.

Jarlsberg Fondue

4 servings

1 clove garlic
2 cups dry white wine – 5 dl
7 cups Jarlsberg, shredded – 700 g
1 tablespoon corn starch
3 tablespoons kirsch or dry sherry
2 teaspoons corn starch
salt, pepper, nutmeg
bread

Use a fondue pot. Rub garlic inside. Heat the wine, do not boil. Mix cheese and corn starch – and drizzle it into the wine gradually. Stir until cheese melts. Mix kirsch and corn starch. Blend into cheese and wine. The consistency should be like a smooth, thick sauce. Season with salt, pepper and a little grated nutmeg.

Cut white or brown bread in cubes. Use fondue forks for dipping the bread.

Jarlsberg Stuffed Fillets

8 servings

1 cup mushrooms, chopped – 2¹/₂ dl
¹/₃ cup green onions, sliced – 1 dl
2 tablespoons butter
¹/₂ cup white bread crumbs – 50 g
2 cups shrimps, cooked and peeled –
    200 g
1¹/₂ cups Jarlsberg, shredded – 150 g
8 sole fillets (about 2 pounds) – 1000 g
1 teaspoon salt
¹/₂ teaspoon white pepper
¹/₂ teaspoon paprika
2 tablespoons butter, melted
2 tablespoons lemon juice

In skillet sauté mushrooms and onions.
Add bread crumbs and 1 cup Jarlsberg.
Add shrimps. Divide mixture among fillets. Roll up. Place seam side down in
buttered, shallow baking dish. Mix salt,
pepper and paprika. Sprinkle over.
Drizzle butter and lemon juice over.

Bake at 400 °F (200 °C) for 20 minutes or
until fish is done.
    Top with remaining ¹/₂ cup Jarlsberg.
Bake until cheese melts.

Jarlsberg Cod

4-6 servings

2 pounds fillet of cod – 1000 g
2 teaspoons salt
$1/_2$ teaspoon white pepper
1 clove garlic, minced
3 medium tomatoes, sliced
1 small leek, thinly sliced (green onion)
2 cups Jarlsberg, shredded – 250 g
$1/_2$ cup light cream or milk – $1^1/_2$ dl

In buttered, shallow baking dish place serving-size pieces of cod. Season with salt, pepper and garlic. Arrange tomato slices and leek over fish. Top with cheese and pour milk over.

Bake at 350 °F (170 °C) 30 minutes or until fish flakes easily and cheese is golden.

Jarlsberg Squares

4-6 servings

4 cups Jarlsberg, grated – 400 g
4 eggs, slightly beaten
$^1/_2$ cup mushrooms, chopped – 100 g
$^1/_4$ cup chives, chopped – $^1/_2$ dl
$^1/_2$ teaspoon white pepper

Combine all ingredients and spread into buttered baking dish.

Bake in preheated oven 350 °F (170 °C) 20 minutes.

Leave for 5 minutes. Cut into 1 inch (2$^1/_2$ cm) squares. Can also be served in portions as a light dinner with crisp salad.

44

Jarlsberg Stuffed Peppers

4 servings

4 cored, green or red peppers
1 pound lean ground beef – 500 g
¹/₂ teaspoon Tabasco sauce
¹/₂ teaspoon garlic powder
¹/₂ teaspoon black pepper
¹/₄ cup lemon juice – ¹/₂ dl
3 slices wholewheat bread, crumbled
2 cups Jarlsberg in half inch (1 cm) cubes
– 200 g
butter – garlic powder (optional)

Mix well beef, Tabasco, garlic, pepper and lemon juice. Stir in breadcrumbs and cheese. Spread evenly in peppers.

Bake on a bed of salt in preheated oven 350 °F (170 °C) 35-40 minutes.

Drizzle with hot garlic butter just before serving.

Jarlsberg Citrus Chicken

4 servings

1 chicken – 1000 g – cut into serving
   pieces
2 tablespoons butter, melted
salt and pepper
1 can cream of mushroom soup
   (10³/₄ ounces) – 300 g
³/₄ cup orange juice – 2 dl
2 cups Jarlsberg, shredded – 200 g
¹/₄ cup green onions, chopped – ¹/₂ dl
¹/₃ cup almonds, toasted, slivered – 1 dl
cooked rice

Place chicken in baking dish. Brush with
butter and sprinkle with salt and pepper.
   Bake at 375 °F (190 °C) for 45 minutes.

Blend together soup, juice, cheese and
onions. Spoon over chicken.
   Bake for additional 15 minutes.

Arrange chicken on hot cooked rice.
Spoon over sauce and sprinkle with almonds.

Jarlsberg Potato Skins

8 servings or 16 appetizers

4 medium baking potatoes, baked
1 cup bacon, cooked crisp and
    crumbled – 200 g
2 cups Jarlsberg, shredded – 200 g
1 egg, slightly beaten
2 tablespoons green chilies
2 tablespoons red pepper
2 green onions, diced
sour cream – chives

Cut potatoes in half lengthwise. Scoop out all but $1/4$ inch (1 cm) pulp. Use scooped-out potato in another recipe. Combine bacon, $1^1/_2$ cups cheese (150 g), egg, chilies, red peppers and onion, blending well. Spread evenly in potato shells. Sprinkle with remaining cheese.

Bake in preheated oven 350 °F (190 °C) 15-20 minutes or until cheese is melted and bubbly.

Serve with sour cream and chives if desired. To serve as appetizers, cut each in half.

48

Jarlsberg Beef Appetizer

6 servings

$^1/_2$ pound beef tenderloin cut into
   matchsticks – 250 g
2 medium tomatoes, diced large
3 cups broccoli, chopped – 200 g
1 large red onion, diced large
1 small green pepper, diced
2 cups fresh mushrooms, chopped – 6 dl
2 cups Jarlsberg, shredded – 200 g
3 tablespoons butter
2 tablespoons soy sauce

4 tablespoons parsley (2 teaspoons dried)
1 teaspoon coarse black pepper
$^1/_2$ teaspoon garlic powder (optional)

Heat butter, soy sauce, pepper and garlic in heavy skillet with lid. Fry beef one
minute at high heat. Add remaining ingredients, except cheese and sauté until
tender – about 20 minutes. Sprinkle
cheese over to cover thickly. Replace lid
and simmer until cheese melts into mixture – 3-4 minutes.

Serve immediately with a crusted
bread.

Jarlsberg Salmon Mousse

8-10 servings

1 can condensed cream of mushroom
   soup
$^1/_2$ pound cream cheese – 250 g
2 cups Jarlsberg, grated – 200 g
1 envelope unflavoured gelatin
1 cup mayonnaise – 200 g
1 pound salmon, cooked – 500 g
$^1/_3$ cup onion, finely chopped – 1 dl
1 clove garlic, pressed
$^1/_4$ teaspoon white pepper
2 teaspoons horseradish, grated

In saucepan combine soup, cheese and
gelatin. Cook over medium heat until
melted. Remove from heat, cool a little
and add remaining ingredients. Stir until
well mixed.

Pour into greased molds and chill.
Unmold and serve on bed of lettuce.

Decorate with peeled shrimps, dill and
lemon.

JARLSBERG THE SNACKING CHEESE

Hungry between meals?

Yes, a lot of us are, and we want something to nibble. Nutrition-wise cheese is probably the best you can eat between meals.

And if you add a little fruit or vegetables you are in perfect balance as far as nutrients are concerned. Jarlsberg is the perfect nibbling cheese –

- in the morning, if your breakfast was not satisfying
- an «after-school-snack» – when the youngsters are waiting for their dinner
- as cocktail snacks
- late at night when your stomach is pleading for something special

Have fun with your favourite cheese.

Jarlsberg Pizza

6-8 servings

1 package dry yeast
³/₄ cup lukewarm water – 2 dl
2 tablespoons oil
¹/₂ teaspoon salt
2 cups flour – 300 g
¹/₂ pound sausage meat – 250 g
2 tablespoons butter
2 cups mushrooms, sliced – 5 dl
4 large tomatoes, diced large
1 green pepper, cut into strips
1 teaspoon oregano
2 cups Jarlsberg, shredded – 200 g

In bowl dissolve yeast in water. Add oil and salt. Stir in 1 cup flour. Beat until smooth. Stir in enough remaining flour to make soft dough. Let it rise until doubled.

In skillet sauté sausage meat in butter. Stir until it breaks into bits. Add mushrooms, tomatoes and pepper. Sauté 10 minutes.

Roll dough out to a large 15 inch (40 cm) circle on baking sheet, forming ¹/₂ inch (1 cm) rim around edge.

Bake at 450 °F (250 °C) for 5 minutes. Pour over sausage sauce. Sprinkle with oregano and cheese. Bake at 425 °F (ca. 210 °C) for 15-20 minutes or until crust is golden and cheese is bubbling.

Jarlsberg Ham and Onion Pie

4-6 servings

Pastry:
2 cups flour – 300 g
1 teaspoon salt
$^1/_2$ cup butter – 150 g
1 cup Jarlsberg, shredded – 100 g
2 tablespoons ice water

Filling:
2 onions, chopped
2 tablespoons butter
$1^1/_2$ cups cooked ham, chopped – 250 g
4 eggs, beaten
1 cup whole milk – $2^1/_2$ dl
2 cups Jarlsberg, shredded – 200 g
$^1/_2$ teaspoon pepper

Combine flour and salt. Cut in shortening using pastry blender. Stir in cheese. Add water one tablespoon at a time until mixture leaves sides of bowl and forms a ball. Divide in half and roll out to fit bottom and lid for pie.

In skillet, sauté onion in butter.

Add ham. Mix all ingredients for filling and place in pastryshell. Place remaining pastry on top. Crimp and seal edges. Decorate with strips of pastry. Brush with egg.

Bake at 425 °F (225 °C) for 40 minutes or until crust is golden.

Jarlsberg Vegetable Bake

6 servings

1 medium eggplant, sliced
$^1/_2$ cup oil – $1^1/_2$ dl
3 medium zucchini, sliced
1 cup mushrooms, sliced – 3 dl
$^1/_2$ cup green peppers, cut in strips –
    $1^1/_2$ dl
$^1/_2$ cup green onions, sliced – $1^1/_2$ dl
1 cup cherry tomatoes, halved – $2^1/_2$ dl
1 teaspoon salt

$^1/_4$ teaspoon pepper
2 cups Jarlsberg, shredded – 200 g

In skillet sauté eggplant in oil, browning lightly on both sides, set aside. Sauté zucchini, mushrooms, peppers and onions for 5 minutes. Add tomatoes, salt and pepper.

Alternate layers of vegetables and cheese in shallow buttered baking dish. Cheese on top.

Bake at 350 °F (170 °C) for 30 minutes.

Jarlsberg Quiche

4-6 servings

Pie shell:
$1^1/_2$ cups flour – 200 g
$^1/_2$ teaspoon salt
$^1/_2$ cup butter – 150 g
2 tablespoons ice water

Filling:
4 eggs
1 cup milk – $2^1/_2$ dl
2 tablespoons chives, chopped
$^1/_2$ teaspoon pepper
2 cups Jarlsberg, shredded – 200 g
$^1/_2$ cup bacon, cooked crisp,
   crumbled (50 g)

Combine flour, salt and butter, using a pastry blender. Add water until mixture forms a ball. Put in 8 inch (20 cm) pie pan.
Bake in preheated oven 400 °F (200 °C) 10 minutes.

In blender combine eggs, milk, chives and pepper. Sprinkle cheese into baked pie shell. Pour over egg mixture. Sprinkle bacon on top.
Bake at 375 °F (190 °C) 30 minutes or until knife inserted in center comes out clean.
Serve immediately.

59

Jarlsberg Breakfast Apple Pie

4-6 servings

3 apples, sliced
$^1/_2$ cup brown sugar – 1 dl
1 teaspoon cinnamon
$^1/_4$ cup butter – 75 g
4 eggs, slightly beaten
1 cup whole milk – $2^1/_2$ dl
1 cup flour – 150 g
$^1/_4$ teaspoon salt
$1^1/_2$ cups Jarlsberg, shredded – 150 g

Arrange apples in buttered pan. Sprinkle with sugar and cinnamon.
   Bake at 350 °F (170 °C) 20 minutes.

Blend remaining ingredients, pour over hot apples.
   Bake 25-30 minutes, or until puffy and golden.
   Serve immediately.

Jarlsberg Soufflé

4 servings

3 tablespoons butter
3 tablespoons flour
1 cup milk – 2¹/₂ dl
1 teaspoon salt
5 eggs, separated
3 cups Jarlsberg, shredded – 300 g

In saucepan melt butter, stir in flour, add milk and cook to thick white sauce. Add salt, egg yolks and cheese. Whip egg whites until stiff peaks form. Stir first ¹/₃ – then the rest – carefully into the cheese mixture.

Pour into greased soufflé dish.

Bake at 350 °F (170 °C) 50-60 minutes.
Serve immediately.

JARLSBERG THE BAKING CHEESE

Jarlsberg Coffee Cake

1 cup sugar – 200 g
3 cups flour, sifted – 450 g
2 teaspoons baking powder
$1/_2$ teaspoon salt
$1/_4$ teaspoon nutmeg
$1/_2$ cup butter – 150 g
2 eggs, beaten
$1/_2$ cup milk – $1 1/_2$ dl
$1/_2$ cup walnuts, chopped
1 cup apples, diced
1 tablespoon lemon juice
2 cups Jarlsberg, diced – 200 g
1 teaspoon cinnamon
2 tablespoons sugar

Combine first 5 ingredients. Work in soft butter. Add egg, milk and nuts. Add apples sprinkled with lemon juice. Finally add cheese. Pour into 8 × 8 inch (24×24 cm) greased pan. Sprinkle mixed cinnamon and sugar over top.

Bake at 375 °F (190 °C) about 25 minutes.

CHEESE YEAST DOUGH

1 cup Jarlsberg, shredded – 100 g
4 cups flour – 600 g
$^1/_2$ teaspoon salt
1 package dry yeast
$1^1/_2$ cups whole milk – 4 dl

Mix cheese, flour, salt and yeast. Add lukewarm milk and mix to a soft dough. Let rise to double size.

Jarlsberg Croissants

24 croissants

Divide into 3 equal parts. Roll each into circles; 12 inches (36 cm). Cut each into 8 equal wedges. Roll up, beginning at the wider end. Bend gently. Let rise 20 minutes. Brush with beaten egg, sprinkle with sesame seeds.

Bake at 425 °F (225 °C) for 15 minutes.

Jarlsberg Rolls

24 rolls

Divide into 24 equal parts. Roll between hands to rolls. Brush with egg, sprinkle with grated cheese. Bake as above.

Holiday Braid

3 small loaves

Divide dough into 9 equal parts. Roll each part into long narrow strips. Join 3 strips at top ends and braid the strips together. Let rise and bake as above (25 minutes).

Whole Wheat Cheese Bread

Use the same ingredients as above, but substitute half of the flour with whole wheat. Let rise to double size. Knead dough – and put one half into buttered sponge cake pan – 8 inches (24 cm) wide.

Cut Jarlsberg in slices and cover the dough. Sprinkle with chopped spring onion. Put rest of the dough on top. Brush with egg and sprinkle with chopped parsley.

Bake at 400 °F (200 °C) 30 minutes.
Serve luke warm.

Jarlsberg Savory Cake

$^1/_2$ cup butter – 150 g
$1^1/_2$ cups Jarlsberg, shredded – 150 g
$1^1/_2$ cups flour – 225 g
1 teaspoon salt
$^1/_2$ teaspoon pepper

Filling:
1 cup cream – $2^1/_2$ dl
1 cup Jarlsberg, shredded – 100 g
3 egg yolks
$^1/_2$ cup Jarlsberg, shredded – 50 g
radishes

In bowl combine first five ingredients to a dough. Leave in a cool place for one hour. Divide into 2 equal parts.

Roll each into circles, 8-10 inches (24-30 cm). Prick with a fork.

Bake in preheated oven 400 °F (200 °C) 10 minutes or until golden and crisp.

Cool on rack.

In saucepan mix cream, cheese and egg yolks over low heat until thickened and smooth. Cool.

Fill cheese cream between cake layers just before serving. Sprinkle cheese on top and put the cake a few seconds under the broiler until the cheese melts.

Serve immediately with fresh radishes.

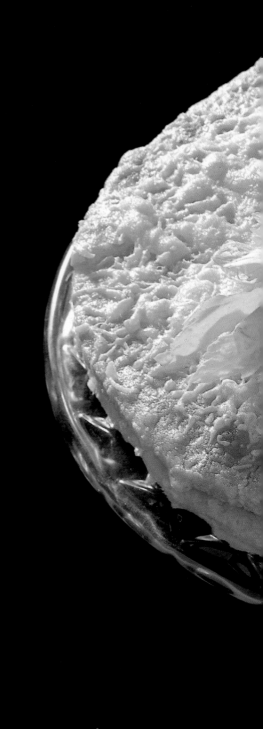

Jarlsberg Sausage Tarts

12 tarts

½ pound pork sausage meat – 250 g
1½ cups flour – 200 g
½ cup butter – 150 g
3 tablespoons cold water
2 eggs, slightly beaten
½ cup light cream – 1½ dl
3 tablespoons green onions, thinly sliced
2 cups Jarlsberg, shredded – 200 g

In skillet, brown sausage meat, stirring to break into bits. In bowl combine flour, butter and water to a soft dough. Press about 1 tablespoon on bottom and sides of 12 greased muffin cups. Sprinkle sausage into each prepared cup. Beat together eggs and cream. Add onions. Divide evenly among cups. Sprinkle a thick layer of cheese over each.

Bake in preheated oven 375 °F (190 °C) 25 minutes or until golden.
   Remove from muffin cups to serve.

Jarlsberg Cheese Rolls

50 rolls

$^1/_2$ cup butter, melted – 150 g
2 packages dry yeast
$1^1/_4$ cups water – $3^1/_2$ dl
3 cups Jarlsberg, shredded – 300 g
4 cups flour – 600 g
1 teaspoon salt
4 eggs, slightly beaten

In bowl combine all ingredients to a smooth, soft dough. Use two spoons and make small rolls on buttered baking sheet. Let rise to doubled size – 1-2 hours. Brush with beaten egg.

Bake in preheated oven at 375 °F (225 °C) 20 minutes.
　　Serve warm. Can easily be frozen and reheated.

Jarlsberg Date and Walnut Bread

1 loaf

1 cup dates, pitted, chopped – 2$^1/_2$ dl
1 cup milk, hot – 2$^1/_2$ dl
2 cups sifted flour – 400 g
2 teaspoons baking powder
1 teaspoon salt
$^1/_2$ cup sugar – 1 dl
$^1/_2$ cup walnuts, chopped – 1$^1/_2$ dl
2 cups Jarlsberg, shredded – 200 g
2 eggs, beaten.

Pour hot milk over dates, set aside.

Combine flour, baking powder, salt, sugar, walnuts and cheese. Stir eggs into date mixture and blend with the other ingredients. Spoon batter into greased pan.

Bake in preheated oven 325 °F (170 °C) about 60 minutes.

Serve hot with butter or sour cream and favorite jam.

Jarlsberg Bacon Bread

1 loaf

6 slices bacon
$^1/_4$ cup green onions, chopped – $^1/_2$ dl
4 tablespoons parsley, chopped
2 cups flour – 300 g
2 teaspoons baking powder
2 teaspoons dry mustard
$^1/_2$ teaspoon salt
2$^1/_2$ cups Jarlsberg, shredded – 250 g
1 cup whole milk – 2$^1/_2$ dl
2 eggs, slightly beaten

In skillet cook bacon until crisp. Crumble. Add onions and parsley to dripping and cook until onion is tender. Add bacon. In large bowl combine flour, baking powder, mustard, salt and cheese. Blend milk, eggs and bacon mixture. Add to flour mixture. Blend until just moistened. Spoon into greased baking pan.

Bake at 350 °F (190 °C) for 50-60 minutes.

Cool in pan 10 minutes. Serve lukewarm with soup.

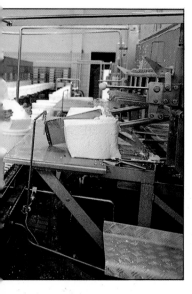

JARLSBERG
CHEESE MAKING

Jarlsberg cheese is produced in five large modern dairies located in various parts of Norway.

Norwegian milk, the raw material, is considered to be among the best in the world, and this is one of the reasons why Jarlsberg cheese is highly appreciated by consumers. The dairies are situated along the fjords of Norway with their cool, clean water.

Pure air surrounds the dairies and the farmland where the cows graze.

These factors combined with skilled, experienced cheese makers are also reasons for the end product's high ranking among cheese connoisseurs.

The Norwegian dairy industry takes great pride in maintaining this top quality image, and every effort is made to ensure the continuation of Jarlsberg as an attractive and much sought after cheese all over the world – from North Cape to Tasmania, from Stockholm to Vancouver and Tokyo.

INDEX